Strategies for Evaluation

Forming Judgments About
Information for Classroom,
Homework, and Test Success

David Wilson

rosen
central ™

The Rosen Publishing Group, Inc.,
New York

For Lauren and Michael

Published in 2006 by The Rosen Publishing Group, Inc.
29 East 21st Street, New York, NY 10010

First Edition

Library of Congress Cataloging-in-Publication Data

Wilson, David, 1974–
Strategies for evaluation : forming judgments about information for classroom, homework, and test success / David Wilson.—1st ed.
    p. cm. — (The library of higher order thinking skills)
Includes bibliographical references and index.
ISBN 1-4042-0473-3 (lib. bdg.)
ISBN 1-4042-0656-6 (pbk. bdg.)
1. Critical thinking—Study and teaching (Secondary) 2. Evaluation—Study and teaching (Secondary)
I. Title. II. Series.
LB1590.3.W545 2006
370.15'2—dc22

                                                                2004030620

Manufactured in the United States of America

On the cover: Portion of *The Thinker* by Auguste Rodin.

Cover (right corner inset), p. 1 © Royalty-Free/Nova Development Corporation.

CONTENTS

INTRODUCTION

When we use a computer, we often take for granted the complicated and powerful processes that make it work. What difference does it make, we might think, how a computer does what it does as long as it does what we want it to do? Of course, if one were going to design a new computer program, one would need to know the ins and outs of how a computer works, but for the rest of us, the results are all we care to see.

It's the same thing with our minds. We think and solve problems, but often we don't care about the process behind our thinking. We only need to know that we have arrived at the desired result. This is all well and good as long as we are happy with our ability to think and solve problems. But what if we want to improve our thinking and problem solving skills? In order to do this, we must look a bit deeper at how we think.

Like the computer, our thinking skills are deceptively complex. To get an idea of this complexity, we can break thinking down into a number of different skills. Thinking begins with collecting information, or knowing what the facts are. This is a fairly straightforward task and is something you are already familiar with. Then thinking starts to get more complex. After you collect information, you need to understand the information—you need to know what it means and why it is important. Then, you need to know how to apply the information, or use it in new situations. Another important thinking skill is known as evaluation, which is making judgments about information or ideas. This book examines both real-world examples and school and test-related examples where you will be asked to evaluate.

Evaluation can be used in every subject and discipline. This skill is probably already familiar to you, whether you realize it or not. But why is evaluation important? It's important because by learning more about the skill of evaluation, you'll increase your chance of doing well at school. It can also lead to success outside of school, or anywhere you are asked to make thoughtful decisions.

Finding Similarities and Differences

One way to evaluate is to find the similarities and differences between two things. For example, if you were asked to describe in a few sentences the similarities and differences between a dog and a cat you might come up with something like this:

> Both dogs and cats have fur, four legs, and a tail. However, a dog barks while a cat meows. Also, many dogs like to swim, but cats don't like to swim.

Sometimes, though, it might not always be obvious when you are being asked to evaluate. Often, test questions use key words other than "evaluate" or "find the similarities and differences." A few of these key words are "appraise," "compare," and "select." In this chapter, we'll discuss these key words in more detail.

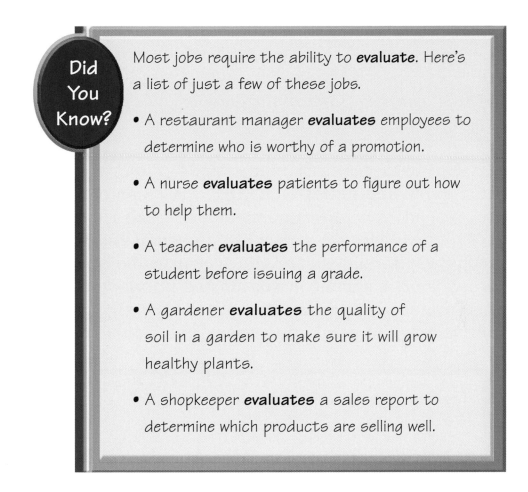

Did You Know?

Most jobs require the ability to **evaluate**. Here's a list of just a few of these jobs.

- A restaurant manager **evaluates** employees to determine who is worthy of a promotion.

- A nurse **evaluates** patients to figure out how to help them.

- A teacher **evaluates** the performance of a student before issuing a grade.

- A gardener **evaluates** the quality of soil in a garden to make sure it will grow healthy plants.

- A shopkeeper **evaluates** a sales report to determine which products are selling well.

Appraise

"Appraise" means to estimate the quality of something. For example, teachers use scoring guidelines to appraise student work. In writing assignments and tests for language arts, these guidelines are used to determine whether students meet the requirements for good writing. After having you review the guidelines, a language arts teacher might give out sample essays and the following assignment:

Using your knowledge of the grading guidelines, appraise each essay as passing or failing.

This task requires many skills. First, you must know and understand what the guidelines are. Second, you must understand how the rules of the guidelines are applied to an actual essay. Once these conditions are met, you must be able to use your judgment, based on the information and evidence, to appraise the essays as meeting or not meeting the standards set for passing papers.

Try It!

Find two old writing assignments. Neither writing assignment should have received a grade. Your new assignment is to **appraise** the writing by assigning a letter grade to each piece. On a separate sheet of paper, write a short paragraph detailing why you decided on the grades for each piece of writing. In your paragraph, make sure you include the criteria you used to **appraise** the writing, such as spelling, grammar, structure, or vocabulary.

Compare

"Compare" means to examine in order to find similarities or differences. Suppose you are interested in buying a pair of shoes. You go to the shoe store and find that there are two pairs of shoes in your price range. You could randomly pick one or choose one because you have seen others wearing that same kind. However, neither of these methods uses evaluation skills. Instead, the best way to choose would be to compare both sets of sneakers and then decide which pair best suits your needs.

When you compare, you take two items and look at the ways that both items are alike and different. With the shoes, you might find that price, comfort, and appearance

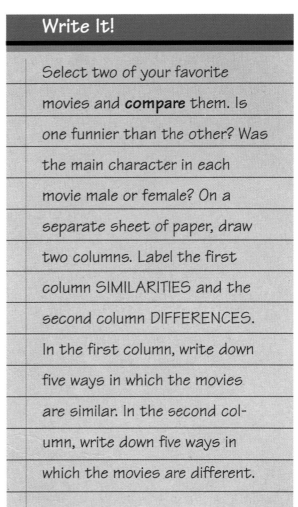

Write It!

Select two of your favorite movies and **compare** them. Is one funnier than the other? Was the main character in each movie male or female? On a separate sheet of paper, draw two columns. Label the first column SIMILARITIES and the second column DIFFERENCES. In the first column, write down five ways in which the movies are similar. In the second column, write down five ways in which the movies are different.

are similar, but that one pair is more suited for tennis and one pair is more suited for basketball. If you plan to use the shoes for one sport but not the other, your comparison would make it easier for you to make a choice.

There are several strategies that are helpful when you are asked to make comparisons. One that you might have heard of is the Venn diagram, which is a diagram of two circles that overlap like chain links. Venn diagrams can be used as tools for comparison by assigning one circle to each thing being studied. When comparing, you would write the similarities of both things in the area that both circles share and the differences in the areas that are not shared. For example, after reading a book for your language arts class, your teacher might give the following assignment:

Compare the characters of Mary and Jennifer.

By designing a Venn diagram, you could more easily complete the assignment. For example, in the shared area you might list "both play the piano," "both are girls," "both are in middle school." In the outer parts of the circles, you might list "has divorced parents," "has red hair," "outgoing," and "hardworking" for Mary and "has black hair," "has three sisters," "shy," and "lazy" for Jennifer. Doing

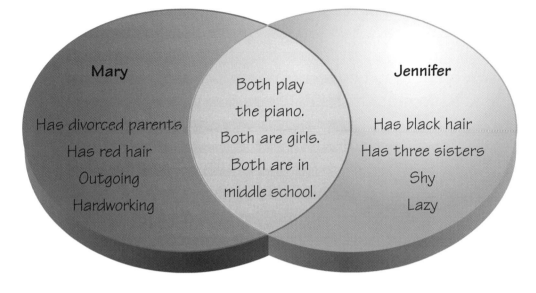

Mary

Has divorced parents

Has red hair

Outgoing

Hardworking

Both play
the piano.
Both are girls.
Both are in
middle school.

Jennifer

Has black hair

Has three sisters

Shy

Lazy

so would make the task of comparing the characters much easier.

Select

When discussing how to compare different things, we looked at the example of buying shoes. After finding two pairs that fit your taste and budget, you had to compare them. Although the act of comparison would allow you to identify the similarities and differences of the shoes, it would not actually result in your choosing a pair and buying them. If you were to choose a pair, you would be selecting a pair, not just comparing them.

"Select" means to make a choice from among several options. When you select an item, you consider the similarities and differences between the items and then pick the one that best suits your needs. Again, using the example of two characters from a book, your teacher might require you to do more than simply compare the characters by giving the following assignment:

If you were a store owner, which character would you select to work in your store?

This task would require you to not only compare the characters, but to use the information obtained from the comparison to make a choice. In this case, you would consider what characteristics you need in an employee. If you were hiring a person to work

Answer It!

From the word list, **select** the correct word to fill in the blank.

Word list: different, similar, identical, short

An equilateral triangle has three sides of _____ length.

Did you choose "identical" from the word list? An equilateral triangle has three sides of identical length.

in a department store, you would list characteristics that are most important in that sort of environment. If the most important characteristics are for that person to be hardworking and outgoing, then you would select the character that has those traits.

Evaluation Helps Decision Making

In your life, you are bombarded with options. By improving your evaluation skills, you are better able to make decisions based on the information you are given. It is likely that you already appraise the value of your options, compare the value or benefit of one option versus another, and use this information to select the option that makes the most sense. Whether you are buying a product, trading baseball cards, or answering a question in school, much of the process used in making your decision is the same.

CHAPTER 2

Evaluating Your Options

An important aspect of evaluation is to be able to assess the value of different options. For example, imagine that your school is about to have an election. Both candidates seem equally suited for the job. However, one candidate believes that students should be allowed to govern themselves and make their own rules while the other believes that students are better off when they follow the rules set up by their teachers and principal. To effectively evaluate which approach is best, you would need to assess or determine the value of both approaches. Several verbs are usually associated with this sort of task and there are many activities that demonstrate this skill. Let's look at a few.

Judge

You have likely heard about the role of a judge in court. The judge is the person assigned to watch over the proceedings in a courtroom and to give a final decision on the case being presented. In this setting, "judge" is being used as a noun to refer to a person. Still, knowing how "judge" is used as a noun should give us some sense of how it will be used as a verb.

Figure It Out

You are looking for a new cell phone calling plan. Plan A costs $20 a month plus 5¢ a minute. Plan B costs $10 a month plus 10¢ a minute. On average, you use your phone 100 minutes a month. **Judge** which calling plan would be the least expensive.

Did you choose plan B? If you did the math, you'd find that plan A costs $25 per month, while plan B costs $20 per month.

The verb "judge" means to form an opinion after careful consideration. This is exactly what a judge does in a court case. A judge watches both sides present their arguments and provide details that support their sides. Then the judge considers the evidence and forms an opinion.

Ideally, you should do the same thing as a judge whenever you make up your mind or form an opinion. Suppose you see an advertisement for a new video game. It looks like the type of game you might like, though it will take most of your savings to buy the game. You decide to hold off on buying it and do some research first. You start by asking friends and classmates about the game. You follow this up by reading a few reviews on the Internet. Perhaps you even play the game at your friend's house. Once all these steps have been taken and you have given the purchase careful consideration, you are ready to judge whether it is worth your money.

Often, you'll receive assignments at school that ask you to judge. Suppose your science teacher gives a lecture on animals that thrive in desert environments. Your science teacher might then give the following assignment:

Considering what you know about desert-dwelling animals, judge whether a penguin will be able to survive in a desert habitat.

You would then be required to compare the penguin's characteristics and judge whether those characteristics match those of animals that have proven to be able to survive in a desert environment. Knowing that a penguin does not prefer dry, hot environments like desert-dwelling animals, you would answer that a penguin would not survive in a desert habitat. In essence, you are performing the same task here as with the video game. You are weighing evidence, both pro and con, and then, based on the strength of that evidence, you are forming an opinion.

Try It!

A new principal arrives at your school and makes a number of new rules. **Judge** whether you think these rules are fair.

- Students are not allowed to wear yellow clothing because it is associated with a local gang.
- A student must keep at least a C average to be eligible to participate in a sport or any other extra-curricular activity.
- Any student caught cheating on an exam will be suspended for two weeks. If the same student is caught cheating again, he or she will be expelled.

Rank

Suppose you go to the supermarket with ten dollars. Before you left home, you made a list of things to buy. Your list includes gum, milk, cereal, ice cream, a magazine, and a candy bar.

While you are shopping, you find that you don't have enough money to buy all of the items on your list. What do you do? You could pick the items in no particular order and stop once their total value has reached ten dollars, but those items might not be the ones you want or need the most. Or, you could pick every item on your list and then let the cashier

Answer It!

Horatio wants to know who is the most accurate free throw shooter on the basketball team. Player A has made 38 of 50 free throws. Player B has made 15 of 25 free throws. Player C has made 48 out of 60 free throws. Which of the choices below correctly **ranks** how well the players shoot free throws, from best to worst?

A) A, B, C
B) B, A, C
C) C, B, A
D) C, A, B

The correct answer is D. Player C has made 80 percent of his free throws. Player A has made 76 percent, and player B has only made 60 percent.

decide which things you should buy and which you should put back. Both scenarios are obviously flawed. What you would need to do is rank the items based on how badly you need them, then choose the highest-ranking items that are within your budget.

Perhaps you know that you are going on a long trip the following day and it is important that you have a nutritious breakfast before traveling. Milk

Answer It!

Rank the following states from largest to smallest in area:

Ohio, California, Delaware, Texas, New Jersey.

Considering the states by area, Texas is the largest. California is the next largest, followed by Ohio, New Jersey, and Delaware.

and cereal would be at the top of your list. If your trip was by bus, you might want something to read, and so the magazine would be the next important item. Although you would like gum, a candy bar, and ice cream, they are not as important to you at this moment, so you leave without buying them. You have just ranked the items on your list. In other words, you assigned a value to the items on your list and put them in order of importance.

In school, you will often be called on to show your ability to rank things by value or importance when evaluating them. For example, after a unit on World War I, your history teacher might give the following assignment:

Consider the events leading up to World War I and rank them in order of importance.

To do this, you would first need to know and understand the events that led up to the war. Then, you would need to have some system for determining how important each event was in relation to the war. You might read opinions of historians to help you understand whether the war would have been likely had each event not occurred. Once you examined the evidence and arguments, you would be ready to rank the events in terms of importance.

Prioritize

As noted earlier, when you rank things you place them in order of importance. This is also referred to as prioritizing. You may have heard the word "priority" used before. Often, people will refer to one's priorities, meaning things that are important to a person. Someone might claim that her family is her number one priority, or that her job is her number one priority. What this person has done is

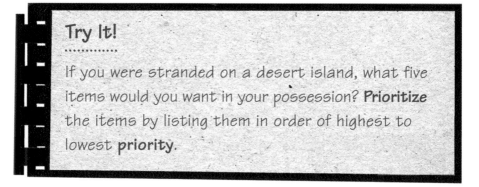

Try It!

If you were stranded on a desert island, what five items would you want in your possession? **Prioritize** the items by listing them in order of highest to lowest **priority**.

considered all of the different elements that make up her life and placed them in order of importance, or priority.

You may sometimes hear prioritize used in place of "rank." It may be helpful to substitute the more common verb "rank" when you encounter the verb "prioritize."

Rate

We previously discussed the verb "appraise." "Rate" is a similar verb. Rate means to determine the value of something in relation to similar items. For example, a friend might say, "On a scale of one to ten, one being the lowest, how would you rate that roller coaster?" Your friend has given you a scale to rate all the roller coaster rides you have taken and asked you to place the roller coaster in question on that scale. If it were the worst one you had ever been on, you would give it a one. If it were the best you'd been on, you would give it a ten. If it fell somewhere in

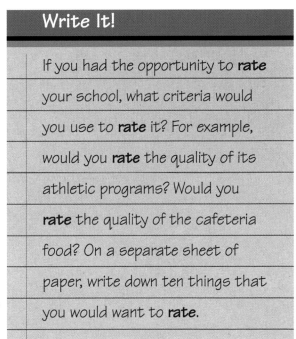

Write It!

If you had the opportunity to **rate** your school, what criteria would you use to **rate** it? For example, would you **rate** the quality of its athletic programs? Would you **rate** the quality of the cafeteria food? On a separate sheet of paper, write down ten things that you would want to **rate**.

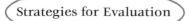
between, you would need to determine how you were going to place it within that range.

A music teacher might present you with the task of rating a song based on a series of criteria. The criteria might include melody, rhythm, and lyrics. After considering these elements, you would be ready to rate the song. If the song in question scored well for all criteria, you would rate it higher than if it only scored well for one or two of the criteria.

It's Your Decision

Life would be easy if every decision we had to make involved a right choice and a wrong choice. You have probably found that this is not always the case. Often, two different options are both appealing. Perhaps a friend is having a party on the day your family has planned to go to the beach. Both options would be fun, but you have to pick. Or perhaps you are trying to answer a multiple-choice question on a test and more than one answer appears to be correct. As you have read in this chapter, a variety of skills can help you make such decisions. In the next chapter, we'll look at more skills that can help you evaluate information and make the best choice.

Making Smart Choices

When we discussed the verb "select," we touched on an important aspect of evaluation—the ability to make an informed and educated choice. This is obviously an important skill. In everyday life, you are constantly being bombarded by choices. For example, you choose what products to buy, what people to hang out with, what movies to see, and what TV shows to watch. If you are not able to evaluate your options, you will rely on luck to decide, or you will leave your decisions to others.

By developing your skills of evaluation, you are better able to make informed choices from among your many options. Thus, you can determine which products might best suit your needs, which friends share the same interests and values as you, which movies are worth spending your money on, and which TV shows are worth your time.

Choose

When we select something, we make a choice. In other words, we choose one item or idea over another. You already make choices in your everyday life, often using fairly complicated thinking skills to do so. If you are invited to two parties on the same day, you must choose between the two by considering the reasons for and against going to either party. In a school election, you would have to choose between at least two candidates.

Answer It!

The Bill of Rights consists of how many amendments?
Choose the correct answer below.

A) Six
B) Ten
C) Fifteen
D) Twenty

Hopefully you answered B. The Bill of Rights consists of the first ten amendments to the U.S. Constitution.

The important thing to remember is that whether taking a test or performing a task in class, proper evaluation requires you to consider the information presented based on a set of criteria or guidelines.

One of the most common examples of such a problem is a multiple-choice question. If you are asked, "Which of the following best describes the theme of the novel?" and five options are listed, you are being asked to choose the correct answer. You will be deciding that one option is better than the other four.

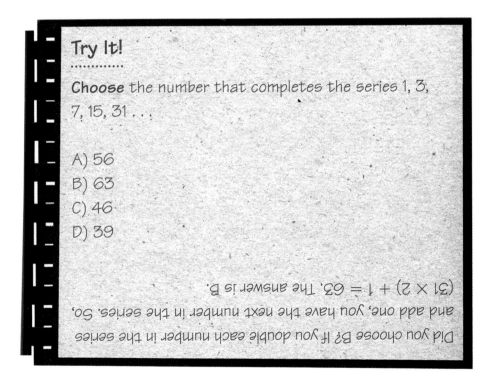

Try It!

Choose the number that completes the series 1, 3, 7, 15, 31 . . .

A) 56
B) 63
C) 46
D) 39

Did you choose B? If you double each number in the series and add one, you have the next number in the series. So, $(31 \times 2) + 1 = 63$. The answer is B.

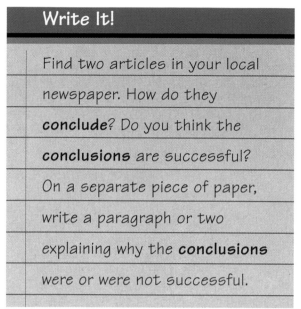

Write It!

Find two articles in your local newspaper. How do they **conclude**? Do you think the **conclusions** are successful? On a separate piece of paper, write a paragraph or two explaining why the **conclusions** were or were not successful.

Conclude

You've likely heard the word "conclusion" used in connection with an essay or a novel. Novels reach their conclusion, in which all of the loose ends come together and everything is made clear. Essays have conclusions in which all of the ideas presented in the essay are restated and some sort of final observation or judgment is made. A conclusion is the end or finish. The verb "conclude" means to reach a decision or form an opinion. Whenever you make a decision on a subject, you are reaching a conclusion.

The following is an example of how your ability to conclude might be tested in a science assignment:

Considering the results of the experiment, what can you conclude about the effectiveness of this technique?

This task requires you to analyze the results of an experiment, determine whether the experiment did what it was intended to do, and, ultimately, conclude whether the technique being used was successful.

Decide

The verb "decide" is often used in place of "choose." In fact, the two are almost identical in meaning. Decide means to make a judgment. When you are

Answer It!

Your friend Carla asks you if you want to go to the movies. You would like to go, except you've promised your sister that you will help her with her homework. What would you **decide** to do?

A) Go see the movie. Your sister will be fine without your help.

B) Tell Carla that you can't go to the movies because you have to help your sister.

C) Don't help your sister and don't go to the movies.

D) Tell your sister go to the movies with Carla while you stay at home and watch television.

E) None of the above

If you've chosen "none of the above," what would you do instead?

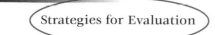

asked to decide, you are being asked to consider the evidence for and against something and then make a decision or judgment.

Let's look at an example in which you are asked to decide. On a standardized math test, you may encounter the following question:

> *Mark needs three bricks to finish the sidewalk out-side his house. He visits the hardware store and finds that bricks are selling for $1 apiece and $5 per half dozen. Decide which would be the best choice for Mark.*

To decide, you must evaluate Mark's needs and determine which makes more sense. In this case, you may decide that, although Mark is getting a better deal if he buys half a dozen, he will be spending two dollars more than necessary and taking home three more bricks than he needs. By applying such logic, you are able to decide what is the best choice for Mark.

Defend

In sports, you often hear about offense and defense. If you are familiar with soccer, you may know that the goalie is the player who is responsible for pro-tecting the net. In essence, that is exactly what you do when you are asked to defend a position or an idea—you must keep that position protected. The verb "defend" means to support or justify. When you are asked to defend a position or an idea, you are being asked to justify it, explain why it is valid, and protect it from being discredited.

Suppose there is a proposal to require all students in your school district to wear uniforms. Arguments have been made for and against school uniforms. In fact, quite a bit of debate has surfaced about the topic. Imagine that your teacher gives you the following essay assignment:

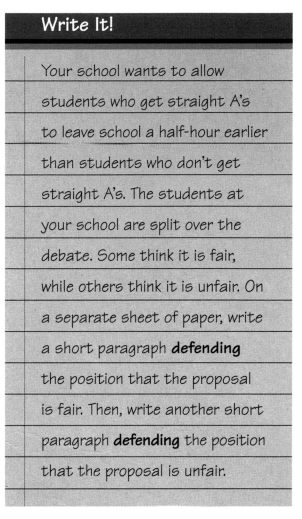

Write It!

Your school wants to allow students who get straight A's to leave school a half-hour earlier than students who don't get straight A's. The students at your school are split over the debate. Some think it is fair, while others think it is unfair. On a separate sheet of paper, write a short paragraph **defending** the position that the proposal is fair. Then, write another short paragraph **defending** the position that the proposal is unfair.

State and defend your position on the debate concerning school uniforms.

In this assignment, there is no right or wrong answer; your ability to defend your answer is the important thing. For example, you might believe that uniforms discourage individuality and that it is unfair to prohibit students from expressing themselves. If you were able to defend your stance with strong arguments, you would be displaying your ability to evaluate information, state a position, and defend your position. Likewise, you might believe that school uniforms make students act more professionally, help families save money, and help school officials determine whether outsiders are in the school. Those are valid arguments too—as long as you state your position clearly and defend it with solid evidence.

Give Your Opinion

We give our opinions constantly. When we talk about movies or sports, we are likely advancing our opinions. In the case of a movie, when you state your opinion you are giving your thoughts based on special knowledge. In this case, you would have special knowledge because you have seen the movie and you have seen other movies to compare it to. From this standpoint, you are prepared to give an honest and educated opinion about the value of the movie. In the case of sports, you may give your opinion on who you think is the best team in the league. You may choose to strengthen your opinion by using statistics, such as comparing win/loss records for all the teams in the league.

When you give your opinion, you are doing so after evaluating the evidence. It is important to note that "opinion" is often used to refer to a personal belief that does not require special knowledge. When giving your opinion on a test or on classwork, it is important to rely on knowledge and facts to back up your opinion.

You may be asked to give your opinion in any subject. Most common, though, you will be asked to do so in language arts and history classes. These classes lend themselves to opinions because you are often reading or studying choices people have made. After considering the reasons for these choices, it is helpful and often interesting to consider whether you agree with those choices. Consider the following assignment:

In your opinion, did the United States make the correct decision during World

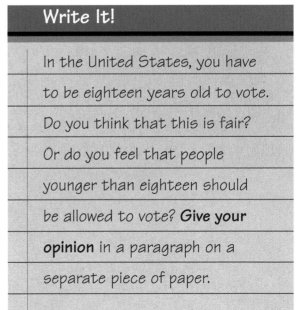

Write It!

In the United States, you have to be eighteen years old to vote. Do you think that this is fair? Or do you feel that people younger than eighteen should be allowed to vote? **Give your opinion** in a paragraph on a separate piece of paper.

*War II to drop atomic bombs on Hiroshima and
Nagasaki in Japan?*

In order to provide your opinion, you would
first need to understand the conditions at that
point of the war. You would also need to understand the reasons for using the bombs as well as
the arguments against using the bombs. Once this
information is understood and analyzed, you will
be able to give an educated opinion as to whether
it was the correct choice to make.

Life Is Full of Choices

At some point, you have probably heard someone
say, "Life is full of choices." Without a doubt, this is
true. When you wake up in the morning, you have
to decide what you are going to wear, what time
you are going to leave, and what you are going to
eat for breakfast.

Throughout your day, you make countless
choices and provide your opinion countless times. It
may seem like you are making these decisions without a complicated thinking process, but you are not.
You are using information, processing it, and weighing its value when deciding what to do. These are
the same skills used in the classroom and on tests.

In the future, when you are faced with choices
or questions in an academic task, take the time to

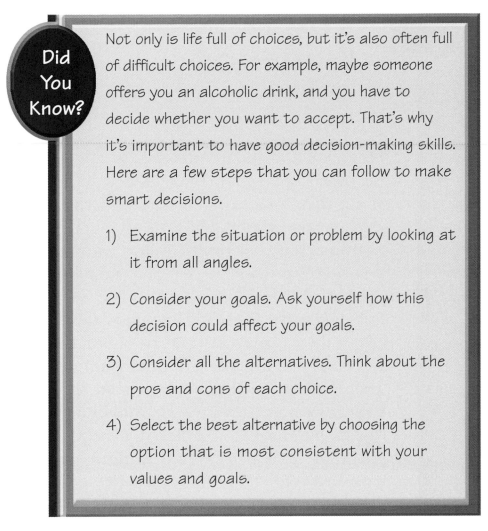

Did You Know?

Not only is life full of choices, but it's also often full of difficult choices. For example, maybe someone offers you an alcoholic drink, and you have to decide whether you want to accept. That's why it's important to have good decision-making skills. Here are a few steps that you can follow to make smart decisions.

1) Examine the situation or problem by looking at it from all angles.

2) Consider your goals. Ask yourself how this decision could affect your goals.

3) Consider all the alternatives. Think about the pros and cons of each choice.

4) Select the best alternative by choosing the option that is most consistent with your values and goals.

think about what you are being asked to do. Likely, it is not that different from what you've already done many times before.

4

Evaluating Evidence

Opinions and judgments should always be based on evidence. Evidence is the proof that something is true and valid. Because we rely on evidence so much, it is important to be able to evaluate whether the evidence we've gathered is credible or not.

Often, the job of evaluating evidence is made more difficult because the evidence may be biased, or prejudiced. For example, in a school election, one candidate may provide a number of facts which back up her belief that schools run more smoothly when students are free to develop their own rules. However, there may be a number of facts that support exactly the opposite position. The candidate may choose not to talk about that information. This candidate would be showing a bias by only showing you part of the available information.

Additionally, it is important to consider the origin of the evidence. If the

Try It!

Carla is writing a report on how pollution is affecting her town. She went on the Internet and searched for information on the subject. She found some good information, but not enough for her entire report. Besides researching on the Internet, can you think of three other ways Carla might find information for her report?

candidate only gave evidence that came from one source, you would be right to be suspicious. Or if the candidate only gave opinions provided by her aunt who lived three states away and was impossible to track down to confirm her opinion, you would be right to be skeptical of the evidence. Also, perhaps the candidate is giving information that isn't relevant to the question of school rules. Although it might be good and accurate information, it might not always be of value in forming a decision on the question at hand. To show fully developed evaluation skills, you should be able to verify the value of evidence and to recognize bias or subjectivity.

We have all been guilty of distorting evidence to support our views at one time or another. For example, when you are arguing that your favorite sports team is better than your friend's favorite team, you are likely to support your claim by carefully choosing what facts you use. Although there may be facts that point toward the other team's superiority, you would not include those facts in your argument. This sort of selection is a fairly complicated thinking skill, and it requires excellent evaluation skills to detect when other people are doing it.

Finding Reliable Sources

Throughout your academic career, you will be called on to do research for classwork, homework, research papers, and other projects. Years ago, most research was done using reference books or periodicals in the library. One could rely on the accuracy of most research because it came from reliable and known sources. That's not to say that one didn't have to be critical of the information, but one could at least trust the source to a certain degree.

In the 1990s, the Internet revolutionized how students conduct research. Now, instead of traveling to the library, you are likely to conduct a large portion of your research via the Internet. The Internet has changed our society in many ways. One of the most powerful ways is that the Internet has allowed anyone with technical know-how to put up content for public view. Although easier access to information is a good thing, it has also required us to become better at evaluating the

Did You Know?

You can ask yourself several questions in order to determine how reliable your sources of information are. They include:

- Does the person providing this information have any reason to distort the facts? (If so, then it's best to find a different source.)

- Where does this information come from? From another source? Or is it personal opinion? (Facts from experts are better than opinions from people who don't know the topic as well.)

- Are there any questions I'd like answered that aren't addressed in this information? (If you have too many unanswered questions, then your source probably isn't doing a good enough job covering the topic.)

value of a source. Who is to say that the information you are using wasn't written by someone with little knowledge of the subject? Or perhaps the studies cited in the article were never conducted. Now more than ever it is important to be able to judge the value of our sources of information.

Did You Know?

Several things need to be considered when determining the value of information on the Internet:

- What is the source? Is it a respected journal or news organization, or is it a personal Web page or blog?

- Who is the author? Can I identify the author or is it anonymous? Can I locate other articles by the author on the Internet? Does the author have any training or experience that makes him or her an expert on the topic?

- Are the statistics and studies referenced accurate? Can I find the same information referenced in other sources? Using the Internet, can I find the original source of those statistics and studies that are being referenced?

Being able to evaluate information and verify the value of sources will ensure that your academic work is based on relevant and accurate research. This is a skill that will not only serve you well in school, but will also help you become a more informed citizen and consumer.

Wrap Up

The skills discussed in this book are not new skills for you, but rather new ways of looking at processes you already perform without knowing it. If you were asked to make a choice or to rank your preferences in something related to your social life, you would probably find that easy to do. When such tasks are asked in an academic setting, however, they can become daunting and difficult.

This book has hopefully made some of these tasks less intimidating and made you realize that you already possess many of these highly developed skills. Now it is time for you to practice and sharpen these skills. With dedication and effort, you're likely to see improvement in your classwork, homework, and test scores.

GLOSSARY

appraise To estimate the quality of something.

bias A tendency to misrepresent or distort the facts about something.

blog An online diary or journal.

choose To select from a number of possible alternatives; to pick out.

compare To examine in order to find similarities or differences.

conclude To reach a decision or form an opinion about something.

credible Capable of being believed.

decide To make a judgment.

defend To support or maintain, as by argument or action; justify.

discriminate To see the differences between similar objects or ideas.

evaluate To examine and judge carefully.

formulate To put into a formula or a system.

habitat The place where a plant or animal lives.

judge To form an opinion or estimation after careful consideration.

justify To demonstrate or prove to be just, right, or valid.

periodical A publication, such as a magazine, that comes out in regular time intervals.

prejudiced Resulting from an opinion based on insufficient facts.

prioritize To place in order of importance.

rank To give a particular order or position to something; to classify.

rate To calculate the value of.

select To make a choice from among several; to pick out.

subjectivity Personal opinion that may or may not be factual.

support To provide evidence for.

WEB SITES

Due to the changing nature of Internet links, the Rosen Publishing Group, Inc., has developed an online list of Web sites related to the subject of this book. This site is updated regularly. Please use this link to access the list:

http://www.rosenlinks.com/lhots/stev

FOR FURTHER READING

Coman, Marcia and Kathy L. Heavers. *How to Improve Your Study Skills*. New York, NY: Glencoe/McGraw Hill, 2001.

Ernst, John. *Middle School Study Skills*. Westminster, CA: Teacher Created Resources, 1996.

Gilbert, Sara Dulaney. *How to Do Your Best on Tests*. New York, NY: Morrow, 1998.

Jensen, Eric. *Student Success Secrets*. Hauppauge, NY: Barron's, 2003.

Nuzum, Margaret. *Study Skills That Stick*. New York, NY: Scholastic, 2001.

Opie, Brenda. *Decimals, Percentages, Metric System, and Consumer Math: Reproducible Skill Builders and Higher Order Thinking Activities Based on NCTM Standards*. Nashville, TN: Incentive, 1995.

Rozakis, Laurie. *81 Fresh and Fun Critical Thinking Activities*. New York, NY: Scholastic, 1998.

BIBLIOGRAPHY

American Red Cross. "Health and Safety Tips: Decision-Making Skills for Young People." Retrieved January 2005 (http://www.redcross.org/services/hss/tips/decision.html).

Arizona State University. "Activities at Various Cognitive Levels of Learning." Retrieved December 2004 (http://ceaspub.eas.asu.edu/MAE-EC2000/blooms.htm).

Ascension Public Schools. "Core Curriculum Guide." Retrieved December 2004 (http://www.apsb.org/schools/allcourses/courses-curriculum.htm).

Bergman, Floyd L. *The English Teacher's Activities Handbook*. Boston, MA: Allyn and Bacon, Inc., 1976.

Fowler, Barbara. "Critical Thinking Across the Curriculum Project." Longview Community College. Retrieved December 2004 (http://www.kcmetro.cc.mo.us/longview/ctac/blooms.htm).

Hooah 4 Health. "How to Develop Your Decision-Making Skills." Retrieved January 2005 (http://www.hooah4health.com/spirit/decisions.htm).

Marzano, Robert J. *Designing a New Taxonomy of Education Objectives*. Thousand Oaks, CA: Corwin Press, 2001.

Medical College of Georgia. "Bloom's Taxonomy of the Cognitive Domain." Retrieved December 2004 (http://www.webcthub.mcg.edu:8900/Hub/NEWHUB/PeerReview/BloomsTaxonomy.htm).

Mt. Edgecumbe High School. "Blooms Cognitive and Affective Taxonomies." Retrieved December 2004 (http://www.mehs.educ.state.ak.us/blooms.html).

Purdue University School of Education. "Evaluation." Retrieved December 2004 (http://education.calumet.purdue.edu/vockell/edpsybook/bloom/evaluation.htm).

INDEX

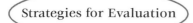
About the Author

David Wilson is a high school English teacher in New Jersey. He received his BA in English from Rutgers College and his MFA in creative writing from New School University.

Designer: Nelson Sá; Editor: Brian Belval